Hyacinths from the Wreckage

Poems

Madeleine Beckman

Hyacinths from the Wreckage

Poems

Madeleine Beckman

Serving House Books

Hyacinths from the Wreckage

Copyright © 2015 Madeleine Beckman

ISBN: 978-0-9862146-5-3

Cover art: Roberto Coromina, "En movimiento" 2015, Steel sculpture

Serving House Books logo by Barry Lereng Wilmont

Published by Serving House Books
Copenhagen, Denmark and Florham Park, NJ
www.servinghousebooks.com

Member of The Independent Book Publishers Association

First Serving House Books Edition 2015

When the past is recaptured by the imagination,
breath is put back into life.
– Marguerite Duras

Acknowledgements

I'd like to thank the following institutions for their support:

Fundacíon Valparaíso, Ragdale, Irish Arts Council (Achill Island), Virginia Center for the Creative Arts, Lerman Trust, and the Writers Room (NYC) for undisturbed time to write.

M.B.

Some of the poems in this book appeared in the following publications:

Whiskey Island Magazine (Cleveland State University), *Confrontation* (Pace University), *Tempus: A Journal of the Arts & Humanities* (Penn State University), *Fetishes* (University of Colorado), *Tattoo Highway, Eight Million Stories, 2 Bridges, Synesthesia, Mother Nature's Trail, A Narrow Fellow, Hinchas de Poesia, Journal of New American Writing, Barrow Street, Skidrow Penthouse, Salonika, Reflections, Response, Southern Poetry Review, New York Quarterly, Minetta Review, Jewish Frontier, An Anthology of Women Poets, Knowing Stones: Poems of Exotic Places* (Anthology*), Nantucket Anthology*

Some of these poems appear in *No Roadmap, No Brakes* ©Madeleine Beckman, 2015 (Red Bird Chapbooks).

Table of Contents

I.

Philly Automat

You've got to live, she told my sisters and me
as we dressed in crisp taffeta dresses
and *Capezio* black velvet shoes
embroidered with pink rosebuds
bought with money from my grandparents
who probably thought my mother bought bread
and eggs – not fancy shoes, but
she had her priorities   and one
was to treat her children to lunch
at Horn & Hardart's on Chestnut Street.

I'd approach the glass windows
with fists full of nickels and dimes, plunge
coins into slots, watch the doors pop open
to BLT sandwiches, macaroni & cheese
coconut custard pie, rice pudding.

Year after year, my mother sat
like a 1940s film star
her coffee without sugar, her ebony hair
pulled back tight in a shoulder-length ponytail
a black piqué dress and marquisette initial pin
placed high on one shoulder.
She never ate during these lunches
(though she tasted from our plates)
and then, when ready, she'd open her purse
remove the gold lipstick brush
and redraw her lips in Spanish red
without a mirror, but with a steady hand.

Indomitable

for my mother

She was *all* about having fun
even when she had no teeth
and was injecting insulin twice a day
after just finishing most of a key lime pie.

She was about penciling in her eyebrows
doing her lips red, *really* red
making it look as if she'd not really thought
about make-up.

Even when there was no heat
or hot water, no food
no glass in the window frames
she managed a meal of lamb chops
and something elegant, magical
like peach cobbler for dessert.

She loved puffy silk slippers and lace;
long enameled Chinese cigarette holders
frequently dangled from her lips
while cooking (see above).

She believed women should use their brains
without forgetting about eyeliner and eyebrows
girdles and padded bras
if you *had* to.

She was about wearing diamond necklaces
diamond rings, diamond watches
(while cooking)
unless the diamonds were in the pawn shop
(along with the paintings worth anything).

She insisted that her children read
listen to opera
know an *escargot*
from a *grenouille*
and under *no* circumstances
live how she lived
and most of all   *dream.*

She Loved Talking

She was a widow
but never thought of herself in those terms
he was still around   despite being dead.

She hated wearing her teeth, hated the insulin injections
refused discipline, but none of this was new.

Increasingly fewer things gave her pleasure.
but she still loved *Mystery Theater*.
She watched to see if her own conclusion
(what she had discerned the first ten minutes watching)
was correct. It was *always* correct.
That one was too easy, she'd say.

One night while in bed wearing slippers and nightgown
the phone rang
during Agatha Christie's *Peril at the End House*.
She answered   and after listening to the caller
said   *You know, I love talking*
dirty, but would you call back in 20 minutes?
The stranger hung up before she did.

See, she had that kind of tough   that you can't see
but can *feel*.

Cedar Road, 4th Grade

My mother thought it ingenious
to shorten the hem of my lavender taffeta skirt
with a staple gun.

Sharp metal teeth   bit
soft flesh.
My 10-year-old knees screamed
bled with each step
every move took more tender skin
like a slow sacrifice.

What are all those things in your dress?
classmates asked, jeering
Oh, look! She has staples in her dress.
Staples!

After the Christmas party
now home   and out of that dress
mom sat on the couch
a cigarette burning in the ash tray
and having found needle and thread
stitch by threaded stitch
hemmed my sister's dress.

Everyone laughed at my skirt, I told her.
Taking a drag on her cigarette,
she assured, *They're just jealous*
they didn't have staples too.

Blood Sisters

for Marie

At eight, you and I pricked fingers
at my mother's kitchen table
became blood sisters for life.

We played doctor with the neighborhood boys
in your basement – were caught by your mother
who screamed at you and sent me home.

You and I pretended we were beauticians
butchered your little brother's hair
while the next victims waited.

We concocted inedible cookies
of cannon-ball consistency and fed them
to Little Sissy – who ate *anything*.

You and I attended confession
told your priest I was Jewish, but had sinned
(peed in the convent stream – with you).

Now, many deaths and miles away
we're still those girls, half naked
under the sprinkler in summer
waiting for the Good Humor man.

After the Czar
for Anna

On a summer afternoon in July   decades ago
we met at Wanamaker's iron eagle,
a Philly landmark welcoming everyone under its wings,
for my birthday shopping excursion
to buy a diamond ring on South Street, Philadelphia.
It was my grandmother's treat
for my reaching double-digits: 10
a magical number she said
like starting all over again.

Anna knew about starting over again
this woman who in *her* single digits worked
stacking loaves in a Kishinev bread shop
her payment: bread
while the Czar gorged on oranges from the Orient.

Now a wife, mother, grandmother
she wasn't wanting   with a row house
full fridge, Singer sewing machine
and four grandchildren.

I chose a simple design, despite her
saying, *pick something more sparkly.*
No, I said, *I like this one*
a simple yellow and white gold setting
that would serve
if I never got the *real* thing.

Now with box in bag we found a bench
on Chestnut Street
where we sat sharing plump red cherries
from a brown paper bag –
sucking each one from the stem
until not a bit of pulp remained.

That's what she taught me: to taste
savor every morsel life gives   cherish
every opportunity like a fruit
bursting   juicy   sweet
    even the pits delicious.

Seventy Years

Her scent grew
each winter
stronger, denser
deep in darkness
her fur coat
wool
in a cedar closet.

He denied
himself
grapes, Sunday drives
believed with her gone
pleasure was over
laughter a word
in a dictionary
he no longer read
after 70 years.

Language of Loss

Everything is flooded
like the rivers and roads
the week your mother died
in Kishinev.

The roads grew into muddy lakes
over which the mourning men turned
themselves into human bridges
passing her over-head
in a simply hand-hewn coffin.

You, a small boy, walked
miles   forgotten between home and
the burial ground.

The earth   soaked in rain and tears
gives beneath my feet
the way we must give
into the language of the dead
not unlike the silences between lovers.

Valentine's Day

Between breakfast and lunch   I consumed
two chocolate Freihoffer's donuts
a bowl of Campbell's Chicken Noodle Soup
and two Cokes.

I'm out of cigarettes, she yells
handing me a dollar with one hand
painting her toenails blood red with the other.
It's 4 p.m., she's lounging in the white velvet chair
where she fell asleep last night
wearing an apricot chiffon nightgown
and black satin Hollywood starlet slippers.

I turn to leave and   he walks in
from last night   cloaked in February freeze.
I've brought all my girls perfume, he says.
And he has.   The perfume's irrelevant
it's the black velvet panther with green glass eyes
clutching the spray bottle   that pulls me close –
I want to be in someone's paws.

I take my gift, my coffee   and run to my cave
where *Everybody must get stoned*
goes 'round and round, again and
I don't have a clue about anything, except   I know
I'm in love, deeply in love   with Bob Dylan

Only Game In Town

Don't look around at what you don't have
look and see what you've got;
be happy you've a seat on the ferry boat
be happy you don't have to stand.
—Paul B.

When he's got a dollar, he knows how to enjoy it.
My father's a survivor.
Our conversations range from Nicaragua
to gays, to Jackson Pollack's discipline
and Faulkner's drinking. *In Mississippi*
everyone lived in a haze of inebriation
even the beautiful genteel women, he recalls
from being stationed with the Air Force down south.

He talks about Bill Irwin. *He's a genius.*
My father's impressed by genius, others and his own.
He's blessed with a positive eye on life, despite
the blows the years continue to dish out.
And his humor, even in the bleakest times
rises with a brilliance, emitting light
when there is none.
His motto when feeling down is *Get lost in your work*
you must get lost.
We talk about Mondrian and *his* pain.
We both know we're alike – our soaring highs
and plummeting lows.

When he almost died and lay in Intensive Care,
his pale calves and thighs showing
from beneath the pathetic faded hospital gown
I was embarrassed for him –
he'd never have wanted me to see
how fragile and helpless even *he* could become.

You've got to keep going, it's the only game in town –
this passion for *every* moment   keeps him alive
long after anyone else would have given up.

Sunday Brunch

We started out in daylight, my father driving the Pontiac
along the Schuylkill Expressway. I'd watch the scullers
on the murky river   move in a one-two-three rhythm
in unison. No wonder Eakins painted this scene over and over
dipping deep beneath the water, beyond the stroke, splash, skill
of "release and catch," of "set your seat," of focus.

We'd eat lunch at Bookbinders: snapper soup with sherry
grenouille, escargots, and with full stomachs drive back home
past the twinkling lights illuminating the wooden boathouses;
the shells now stacked and neatly tucked away
until the next day when the rowers strong and determined
carried out the boats again   set the oars
locked them in place   to repeat the rhythm of rowers.

Now when I row, I understand the precision of fingers
around the oar handles   squaring and feathering the blades
the upright posture, leaning in and returning
moving efficiently through hundreds of strokes
captured by Eakins' strokes   illustrating a sculler's torso, arms
not just any physique, but one that carves through the currents
                heaves to the finish.

A Great Pass

Hey kid, what are you doing up so late?
Come down, keep your Pop company.

No! Don't change the channel
I'm watchin' the game.

Hey, do your Pop a big favor
grab that gallon of butter pecan

from the freezer, don't forget a spoon
and maybe the walnuts in syrup.

He's stretched on the black leather couch
a furniture monstrosity that sticks to your skin.

He imagines he's still the athlete he once was
pitching baskets, the only whitey on a black team.

I pull up the *Lay-Z-Boy* beside him. The chair
is a huge green *Naugahyde* monstrosity.

We watch football reruns, but I'm OK
despite not understanding the scoring.

Did you see that toss, did you see it! He's jubilant
(doesn't see me picking out all the pecans)

while I'm watching him   watching
watching him passing.

Little Rituals

for my father

You come to life in the candle
a bright shadow, dancing.
I wait for your words, but you're absent
(this time you're not just late).
Get lost in your work, you'd tell me.
It was, is, good advice.
In life you never resembled anything
as flimsy as a shadow, or as illusory.

Be happy you have a seat on the ferryboat, be happy
you don't have to stand, you cautioned. Now,
when I get a seat on the train, your words humble me
to what I have, what I might not have in a moment.

The candle burns through the day and night
it's been flickering six extra hours
(you always had more stamina than most).
I remembered and ran to the market
before the 11 o' clock news   couldn't let the day pass
without lighting the candle – my nod to tradition –
though you often forgot birthdays, anniversaries
to pick me up after dances or a party
but people are imperfect, and that's good
it distinguishes us, teaches us
to accept   and if we're lucky, to love.

City Island Seafood

This is for you, with your toothless smile
sucking in oysters, clams, mussels;
cracking claws of unfortunate lobsters,
shells for the screaming bilingual sea gulls, who
know how to attack the inside of a mollusk
the way a flamenco dancer knows how to strike
his or her shoe against the yielding planks.

This is for you in a housedress, a garment you'd never
be caught dead in around the house, or anywhere else
and yet, you're here wearing it outside on an icy January day
because nothing else is comfortable, everything hurts, except
the Latino kids screaming to our left and their granny
in turquoise hair rollers wearing her housedress
being wheeled around in her wheelchair (like you, only
without rollers, too much of your hair has fallen out or
been torn from its root).

This is for you, this drive from Jerome Avenue, away
from the elevated trains, out through the Bronx to
City Island, almost an oasis, if you don't look too close,
but you can't – what with how your eyes have failed –
the diabetes and all – the all being having to see
for so long. Who wouldn't pray for clouded vision?

This is for you, this approach down the pothole drag, past
Italian restaurants, shipyards, crumbling Victorian homes,
condominiums going up on yet another spit of "waterfront property."

My husband is a saint. There are many things he's not, but
saint is not one of them. He will chauffeur you anywhere:
the cemetery to visit your family, shopping, for an ice cream;
he will talk to you at any pitch to assure you hear,
he will take you to whatever restaurant, wearing whatever
we happen to get you to put on.

I am not a saint.
You would like Lutèce, Le Cirque; we go to City Island
a perfect place, and considering the fog in your head,
the haze over your eyes, this could be Spain or
a Caribbean island you knew so well
at another time, saronged in silk
hiked up revealing calves, thighs
that always sent your husband reeling or
snapping yet more photos.

This is for you, in diapers, black hair pulled back
in a cheap pearl barrette (I wear while washing dishes)
stretch slippers, their gold thread comforting swollen feet, and
God help us, that dress, so ordinary, so un-you.
But it's your birthday and despite the condition you're in
or how they've screwed up your medicines or all the neglect
which no one will admit to – or take responsibility for –
you were happy and most important, alive
sitting in the front seat of the car excited, really excited, about
seafood and the illusion of luxury at the beach in the Bronx,
so far from Philadelphia, so far from lunches at Nan Duskin
(wearing well-tailored gray and plum), eating Poire Belle Hélène
or supine in a nighty on the couch
downing *escargots* at midnight watching Johnny Carson.

This is for you, we told the young man behind the counter
(the one with the tattoos and piercings) that it was your 70th
and could he make a really special dish, even though
none of the plates included every species from scallop
to shrimp; we didn't say you probably wouldn't live to eat dessert,
and well, despite the restaurant being a sort of seafood Taco Bell,
he had a heart or maybe a mother and said sure, why not,
he'd do it for the extra money.

Money was never a problem – and always a problem
and with it one could get and do anything, the same as without it.
That's what you and he taught us, and oh yes
how to really suck out the insides of a lobster, until
not even the gulls can find what had been the essence
of a creature who lives without yielding, until
yielding is not a question; an organism no different from
any one of us because we are all stomping, click-clacking our heels
dancers proud and strong and really, just sucking on each other,
releasing one another and ourselves from pain,
trying to miss the potholes, to see how long we can keep
from leaning (against our wills) until finally, we must yield –
to a stranger, a friend, a French fry fork full of coleslaw
from a paper plate in winter.

This is for you, to that long descent
which was the end
of pain, but possibly, hopefully, lulled
filled with sea-soaked penetrating pleasure.

II.

Cadmium Red

the color of choice
my mouth
lipstick
      filet mignon
my lover   full blast
brain   groin   heart
synapses unmedicated
free range thoughts
uncaged   unclipped
I flip
cadmium yellow
moods turn green
flame   through
orange   white hot
      on fire.

Danger in Union City

I'm spinning like a children's top or *dreidel*
with the letters whirling some indecipherable message
transmitted into the stratosphere that no one will ever read.

Every tendon, every muscle is in spasm
but even more annoying is   I had something
I loved, something tangible.
I just wanted to row, to be on the river
with the autumn leaves bending above me
the unexpected burst of fish into sunlight
and gone again.

That first meeting, well, I almost walked away
rather than speak to you. I was out of there
before I was even in.
Just sculling, that's all I wanted.
I didn't invite you to slither between the sinews of my flesh
to take over every neuron, every breath. Hey,
why not go back to Cuba? Go back to Cyprus?
Back to Russia?
Why did they ever let you through our border?

I can hear some of you, but she didn't *have* to
take him up on that drink? Didn't *have* to say, *Yeah,*
watching the 'Kite Runner' at your place
sounds good… and yes, you're right,
I could have said, *No, sorry, you can't*
have that first kiss, can't …

Is it possible to undo? Possible to pick up before
the collision took place?
I'm too old for this. Don't have the stamina
shouldn't still be getting into these situations
shouldn't be falling for the details of espresso
served in bed before he goes off
in thirty-degree weather to scull on the river
and return to the warmth of the apartment and me.

Being with him – I'm a character in a Marquez story.
Listen, he talks to Napoleon and Josephina his two birds
…*yo tu quiero chicas*… and I want him *more*
and know I have to leave   *fast.* Need to get out
of this novel I keep writing, revising
but refuse to give an ending.

West 11th Street

When friends ask, *Do you miss him?*
I say, *on occasion.*
Who would believe after years
and years sharing one bed
(so delicious at times)
the occasion arises
when I need to scrub my back
and find it's hard
to reach those difficult places.

Erosion

I didn't want to see you any more
but   you were there
Hey, I'm here.
Sometimes I stared back   *hard.*
thinking I'd will you gone
other times   I looked away
ignored you.   You didn't care.
Hey, I'm still here.

Special occasions you showed up
more dynamic than ever.
Then someone noticed, said
You should do something about him.
So, I decided,   yes
then undecided, then   really decided.
Despite your tenacity   I discarded you.

Not without   difficulty
not without moments
of looking back   to find you
almost invisible
as if behind a cloud
of memory that shifts
then reveals   demons   colliding
love gone so wrong.

Beyond Passion

hooked
into each other

not enough   heart
to go around

lunged
at each other

against   each other
against   disappointment

passion
            gone perverse

into something
impoverished   like chalk

only knowing about
            really knowing

            just how empty
empty can be.

Black & Blue

My world is black & blue
      without you
with you
      it was black & blue too.

Just Passing Through

I'm just passing through this body
I realize this when I sweat
in a downward dog, when I scull
on the river or lake, the boat
not moving as fast as I'd like
and all I can do is do what my body
can do.

I'm just passing though this body;
should have realized this when
the horse threw me halfway across the ring
and my feet and legs did that weird death spasm
or when the grooms ran over and asked
Can you move your legs?
I could and did and got back up
the way they say you *must*.

I remember when you left –
you *too* are just passing through
this body   like a last wash
at a laundromat that's now closed
for business. **CLOSED.**

It's not just about the body, not completely
that's a losing proposition, like my neighbor
the tarot reader says, *I'm not really here, I play here*
but I'm not really here.
This attitude gets her through.

She leaves me with the words: *It's not about here*
it's about there. When you're gone you're gone…
like a breakup you both knew was coming
but had to play out
        the best you could.

Black Bass Inn

In the bedroom overlooking the Delaware River
two beeswax candles flicker in the dark
illuminating our flesh in the mirror
of a mahogany dressing table holding personal items:
a silver money clip, a red velvet purse, pearl earrings,
an antique cameo brooch from my ex-husband
(anniversary number 1).
For a moment, I think   he's in the room
these things happen.

We watch from the bed, the Delaware River's
currents   dark, deep, insistent
as my feelings for you.
Your smooth strong fingers traverse my neck
my cheeks   search my eyes.
Are you crying? you ask.
Do you want me to cry?
No response   only
more gentle touching   my ears, my face
as a blind man might   absorbing every curve
even ones *I* don't know.

After you return to Ireland
to your wife I didn't know you had
I readjust to my face in the mirror   altered
by your fingers   their prints
microscopic tattoos
indelible impressions
invisible incisions.

Forecast: No Visibility

I dived in   can't figure out – why
     just yet
still reassembling the pieces   whirling
within Sennen Cove waves
tumbling about in the fog on Tresco
scattered   from Stonehenge to Crouch End.

Driving down A391 you said, *we hadn't gotten there*
yet   meaning   we hadn't disemboweled each other
yet   but give it time   *anything* can happen
     with time
and I gave you all the time   and then some.

You've probably not missed a beat
safe with Sally your GPS, and calendar
chock-full of events to keep you fully occupied
where no air or space can leak
in to the de-oxygenated crawl-space
     who is you.

Here – tossing 30,000 feet up
and 3000 miles away
(bowels haywire)   I begin
making sense of the shards
barely recognizable   that were me.

But, *this* I know: no matter how much
you consume, chart, calculate
     you'll remain   bereft
hauling around a heart   hard
as the serpentinite stone of Lizard
where we walked thick green fields
glorious to me   to you
a nuisance but necessary –
a means to reach the jagged stormy edge
     and we did.

Eccentricities

First came the pens.
Did you use my pen today?
he asked. *Yes*, I came forth.
I like my pen tips up.
I couldn't believe he'd noticed.
This quirk was comical.

Then came the dishes.
I place the dirty ones in the sink
until they call to be washed, but
he has a way to stack: glasses upside down
utensils side by side.
This was a detail, easy to handle.

It seemed we clashed like wild flowers
along the road and rows of terraced roses
still, I liked his quest for order, search for perfection
ability to handle chaos.

But the checkbook almost sent us into war.
I'm content knowing every transaction's been entered
arithmetic correct; balance not overdrawn.
He has a method, *Please enter under columns A and B*
don't use plus or minus signs.
I obliged.

When he said, *I don't fold my socks inside out*
into little balls, I like them side by side folded flat.
I saw the humor, *almost.*

Crane Beach

Just yesterday, we filled that beach bag
bursting with *saucisson*, iced coffee
books read between naps.

Now it's Fall and that canvas sack
hangs dejected, stained with SPF 30
black fly and tick spray
and always ink from a leaky pen.

Maybe I'll scrub it, I think
back to its original brightness,
Google Martha for tips
but not even bleach and sun and
New England home remedies
can return that satchel full of wonder
to its previous state
untarnished –
the way we can never return
to the years before.

After Anna Swir

I lie with my husband in bed.
He asks: *Can I touch it?*
He means my firm, round stomach
the hidden child growing in my flesh.
He moves his hand towards me
as if approaching a *Ouiji* board;
he'd like a message; he'd like hope.

It's another summer Sunday morning
near the sea without humidity, a light breeze
pushes past the pines   slipping
through the screens of the little rental cottage
perfect
as the white miniature roses I planted,
pure as the child growing inside me.

In the morning shower, I bend my head
towards my belly. I'm agile and
can still do this   no problem. I sing
cup my full breasts in my hands
while my husband shaves.
We go through our rituals
none strong enough
to heal
what's to come.

Little One

The wind blows over the plains
of Andalucia.
I dig my toes into the soil
feel the new grass pushing through
still, my heart sinks
deeper than the dry riverbeds
when your face, as it does, appears
unborn, yet bright as any star
in the December night   and
as untouchable.

Los Gatos

1.
The canopy bed, sheer white drapes
tied back by yellow & red bougainvillea
three blossoms to each of four posts –
was poetry created by the maid
who'd visited while we were on the beach
drinking coconut milk with rum;
her fingers tied those tiny knots from stems
light as butterflies   fluttering
leaving messages   few hear.

2.
I stood on the balcony overlooking the sea
watching rows of white lights, strands of pearls
outlining the ocean liner's shape
as it passed through Zihuatenejo
the place of women   imagined
lavish meals, evening wear   laughing.
I turned, entered our room again
closed the door on the warm, soft night
absent of smiles, laughter   absent
        of anticipation.
3.
Earlier that day   on the beach
a young Mayan girl approached
my husband and me
she tried selling us a necklace of shell
and a bright-colored scarf
to wrap around my hips.
She demonstrated how to do this –
I knew I wouldn't. All I wanted
in Zihua   was not to want.

Body Remembers

Who's tumbled on this couch with me?
Whose arms and legs wrapped around my thighs?
My shoulders? Whose tongue licked my lips
searched the crevices of my flesh
left prints in places I've yet to see?
Whose heat and sweat mingled
indistinguishable from mine?
Whose hair remained on my body
as if my own?

Where are those people now?
On other couches? In other beds?
Dust?

All that sweetness is held
in my body's memory   because the body
always remembers   knows
stirs to speak to us   *Remember?*
            it asks?

I wake flushed   not knowing why.
And, despite the bridge between us
utterly blown to bits   decades ago
a residue, a blanket of jaundiced disbelief
remains.

This the body remembers too.

#5 Bus

You can smell it   she adores him.
You can sense the dampness
on her fingertips   brought up from deep
love.   Her white hand
clasps his hand   his arm weighs heavy
on her shoulder   the weight reminds her
soon he'll be gone   but for now
she's pretty sure   *this* is happiness.

She turns her head slightly   breathes in
the fragrance of his hair   now gray;
she's known him since before
white mingled with black.   She's into it
for the long haul.

He rests on me like an animal, she once said.
I didn't ask what that meant   my imagination
is enough.
His complexion is soaked with history
no one knows. He likes it that way.

Awestruck in Manhattan   these two
enjoy this brief ride
on the #5 bus.
Hope is always available   it's free.

It's our stop – West Broadway and Houston.
Is this Houston Street? She asks
taking the lead this time
Yes, I assure her.

They take hands again
walk down West Broadway –
one enormous adventure;
it *could* happen
that thing she's got her eye on –

Force of Nature

He's met his match
a friend says
when I say
I'm not responding.

It's been six months
and I haven't seen him
despite tenacious texts and
flirtatious photos.
We're talking *serious*
restraint on my part.

Let's start with his texts:
You need a massage and to relax
and   I'd like to
and then   cryptic detail
about how
he'd…
This is not strengthening
my resolve
he's aware he's eroding.

It helps to repeat to self
he's hollow as the night
whether in his bed
        or mine.

Why don't you tell him
not to contact you?
a friend asks.
I might want to row on his river
I say, no subtext intended
I mean the river he's made his domain.
He wants to see you,
you want to see him —
what's the problem?

I savor his texts   then
hit *Delete*.

Voltage

Watch out
I'm about to vandalize
every wall outlet, do damage
to every electrical wire
pull out the innards
of every ceiling fixture
dig around blindly in the fuse box
to mess it up   *bad*
but not quite beyond repair.

You'll be dispatched
to my side in the dark,
the deadly tail of Scorpio curling
the *n* of electrician
like a lick of the tongue
while you put things right.

Carnival

This is how it *would* have gone:
I would have asked for the aisle
so I could get out.
That's just the way I roll
always looking for the EXIT.

I would have read, and drank
a glass of red wine
while keeping my hands to myself.
You would be asleep, listening to music
or diddling one of your many gadgets;
electronics is your thing.

At the airport you would have helped
cart my luggage because you're, well
big and strong and even better –
a gentleman when the *other* is tucked away.
We'd be wearing sunglasses and half naked
because it's warmer here and that's how I like it.

At the hotel   you would take care of it *all*
because you've got a soft touch when needed.
It's what you know how to do   well
besides some other things –

Under my t-shirt I'd be wearing red
lace   because I like red and *love* lace
and what better time, better place to wear
underwear out   than *Carnival*
when everyone's dancing and
there is no hour
no minute hand pushing.

Paris Is Always A Good Idea
for A.D.

Paris? and you didn't visit le Louvre?
friends balked.

Le Louvre will remain; Raphael
and the rest   will remain
we however
        are fleeting.

We stand looking at Pyramide du Louvre.
What was Pei thinking?
Alzheimer's, I say. *Alzheimer's*
        set in for sure.

I look at the posters advertising the exhibits
Late Raphael would be nice to see
but we'd never get in.
Not even the young French woman
working at la Cathédrale de Chartres
with her France-wide museum pass
        got in with her parents.

Anyway, le Louvre can't compare
to holding hands, laughing, kissing
the architecture, cafés, book stalls
and wild expanse of us   *here*
overlooking the Seine
                in moonlight.

III.

Achill Rhythm

Mornings, I take breakfast on the cliff
watch shell seekers wrapped in slickers
walk along Golden Strand Beach;
birds fly and dive above the rocky Irish coast
taking breakfast from the sea.

Inside, I wash dishes, sweep turf ashes
from the fireplace, consider dinner, and
the slow seven-mile bike ride to the market
down hills, past Gaelic signs
I don't understand, and back up again.

Outside, fuchsia surrounds my porch
grows thick, fragrant, shields me
from the road and uninvited visitors;
pink red purple primrose keeps my cottage hidden
sweet as a lover's promise.

Mid-day, clouds black as volcanic sand
consume a slice of sun   bring on thunderous rain
goat and sheep   their neon-branded rumps
head for home; horses speed their gallop.

After the deluge, double rainbows crown the Irish Sea.
I return laundry to the line, watch Mount Slievemore
emerge through the thick shifting mist.

Evening, I put up water for potatoes
wash the shells of duck eggs, slather butter
on warm soda bread, listen to the tide
a partner in rhythm.

Art of Fire

You've got it, the real thing. – Margaret

Swollen with heat, ashes lay puffy
in heaps from last night's fire.
It was a long evening   dancing, spitting coyly
licking the innards of the chimney.
It's quite a performance, and a lot of warmth
turf fires provide   if you work it right.

Your hands, callused and split
from hours and hours turning bog,
played with the flames last night.
This is your art   you have no choice
but to stay near
she will die if you stray.

Turf makes you toil   from beginning to end
tending cutting drying
weeks and weeks of unexpected rain
and drying   all over again – and sometimes
nothing plus nothing gives you more nothing.
There is never a guarantee.

No telling if devotion will pay back
but the bog will kiss you with blazing tongues
if stroked to satisfaction   turf will cloak you
in joy   despite the inevitable waning
and ultimate death.

Every man and woman on this island cherishes
the land, his land   a piece of God's wealth
passed down and passed down
no way you say *no.*

You need good turf, says the Bog Man
he has no wife, no companion, no dog
the living bog is his mate.

You can't have a good fire without good turf
they probably gave you wet turf for starters
Mary tells me. Her fire burns day and night.
It's probably not the best turf
fire starter bricks help – lots of it…
advises widow Margaret, she knows
how to keep fires alive – even when they're dying.

Neighbors pass outside my little cottage
gaze at the fire through gauzy curtains
knock on my door, congratulate me
Your fire's going mightily. You built it?
Yes, I say, shaking my head
thinking   *you have no idea.*

Here on Achill Island, I walk the bogs
like everyone, smell Ireland's earth
understand   depending on the angle
eventually   *everything* gives.

Beyond Mt. Cloughmore

Mt. Cloughmore's jagged cliffs morph and survive
the ocean's relentless attacks –
>   the sea *always* finds its way out.

Walking Cloughmore's paths and boulders
I hike through the operatic wind, a requiem shifting
>   nearing screams, consuming my ears.

Fear accompanies me surrounded by emerald green
and blooms – vibrant colors
my feet planted   half hidden
in soft grass   at the edge
where path and precipice merge into sky
>   where I can not go.

I look down
and carved into rock amidst clover:
Ireland loves you
with no reserve   I laugh
>   my echo joining the requiem.

Witch Sky

Three fresh grilled sardines
fill the glazed clay plate
one for each of us   a treat at 6 p.m.
when Andalucia's sky whispers
what tomorrow might bring.   We wait
to learn the prediction: stars yes, rain maybe
moon no.

We eat around the spines, leave the heads
intact   eyes staring at no one
nothing.   We wash down our *tapas*
with tough red wine
feel the wind change direction   away
from the plaza   still higher
to *el Castillo*
        in this steep terraced town.

It was impossible to reach Mojácar
even on horseback…
or so 12th-century history goes   yet
the women still climb surefooted
carrying water home to cook another meal
alchemists mixing   wise
as the dark witch sky
        and as mysterious.

To My Body Screaming

Green clay smeared on my leg (to suck out the demons)
Calmatel cream massaged into my knee (to bring down
    the swelling)
Hot salt rinses for my gums (to clean out the infection)
Hydrogen peroxide washes for my tooth (to calm
    the eruption)
Wellbutrin 200 mg (for my emotions)
Naproxin tablets for shredded cartilage (from too much
    running)
Amoxicillan capsules for something, I forget what (but
    it shouldn't have happened)
Arnica granules for all the bruises (inside and out)
Trazadone gel caps to fall asleep (and forget for a moment)
Ibuprofen pills to ease the cramps (from hell)
and strong Spanish wine to wash it all down.

Garrucha, Spain

Be thankful for the interludes
patches where moss grows
heavy   and memory erases
memory.
Be thankful for the days
you don't fear
when anticipation vanishes
like Fall disappearing into Winter
breath is full beyond breath
sweeter and richer than pollen;
be thankful for the pauses
not present before
when song takes over your voice
when what had just been   reminds you
of moments gone
golden horses' tails flying
writing a script written in the wind.

Rooftops of Cordoba

After the gypsy singers and flamenco dancers packed up
their shoes and castanets and left
we poured sherry dark as earth from the *bota*
following Eduardo through tiled courtyards
past clay jugs used by Greeks to transport
all they called their own but wasn't.

Teresa, Alfonse, Maria, Eduardo and I climbed
the Spanish iron stairs of the ancient building in moonlight
high above *Calle de los Judios*
above white-washed houses and one remaining synagogue
circa 1315 – and all that went before.

I trailed Eduardo's white linen trousers
a beacon in the starless night
laughed at his harmless jokes
quieted to the sounds of guitars
in mosaic doorways.

We moved carefree like fortunate children
dancing, singing, clapping   until
everyone stood tight against each other's hips
drenched in rain turning everything slippery.

My soaked silk dress hugged wet flesh
danger or limitations   long gone
in Borges' moonless Cordoba.

Night in Havana

Lit up in lights, Che watches thousands
dancing in *Plaza del Revolución.*
I'm in bed at *Hotel Nacional de Cuba*
certain I'm dying, sick with a respiratory infection.

I drink orange juice, drink papaya juice, drink
without alcohol. I'd like some alcohol.
I'd like to be at the concert I'm watching on TV
the crowd swaying, screaming, loving
the *hot hot* bands.

Up here on the 5th floor
clapping my hands between chills
and scalding heat
my body's an electric coil –
and for the moment   I *am* Cuban.

A Kind of Freedom

Timbales, clave, conga
tumble from *Plaza de la Revolución*
from bubble gum pink, lime green
mango orange cars cruising
el Malecon   reminders
of an almost forgotten era
from pedal taxis and horse-drawn carts –
tumble in waves from doorways, windows
high above the wide, once elegant avenues
from the backs of bicycles, baby strollers
overcrowded buses, from boom-boxes
speakers mounted on donkeys walking
tobacco fields
from ferries, parks, bars, cafes
butcher shops, the open air market and
the woman selling avocados large as my head
on the street corner   from kitchens
the rocks along the sea where men fish
dream of other coasts, from community centers
pharmacies, the hospital triage
where I wait   one among many, except
I will eventually leave – *really* leave.

Pearl of the Antilles

At Bar Montserrat Caridad sings –
her voice sweet as plump fruit and
even more beautiful than she   at 17.

Her musicians play Cuban love songs
and we dance in cramped quarters
where Hemingway drank
and drank and drank.

I buy Caridad's hand-stamped CD;
she signs the liner notes   writes
her phone number, email address
It's my friend's email, but I'll get it.
She aches to visit the U.S.

like Lazaro the pedal taxi driver
and Gustavo and Mariana and
so many others
who haven't yet slipped through
          and *out*.

Luna Rossa

The man and woman dare not scratch, yawn
twitch on the embroidered *prie-dieu*, where
on their knees   they wait
to be pronounced man and wife
by a priest wearing lavish, hand-stitched satin robes,
wait, despite the deadening heat -
sending their guests into near hallucinations
praying for the service to end
      but it doesn't.

And it doesn't   until
the clergyman, still looking composed – not wilting
like everyone in the pews,
finishes his sermon on – hell and betrayal
in this ancient church – where no breeze visits
no window or door absent-mindedly left ajar.
Chiffon, crisp white shirts, silk ties
turn wet, limp. The men in sunglasses scowl.

Through a door, not wide enough for everyone
to leave as quickly as they'd like, we exit
meander along the cobbled streets, up
and up to the hilltop hotel   where *luna rossa*
grows huge   hangs like a jewel over yachts
ferries, the Bay of Naples below this rooftop paradise.
And the blood orange moon   suspended
casts a glow up the coast   beyond champagne
Campari, Italian undulating from tongues
like song sailing on the sea to Capri
that tiny, resilient island   where days later
I learn Pavarotti's dead and *la luna rossa's* long gone.

Rue d'Ormesson

I want something simple.
Go to England said Gertrude, Madam's lover.
Madam, a lady, said, *No, come in.*
What will you have?
Rabbit. Do you have rabbit?
The French like beef, Madam informed me.
They're not interested in rabbit.
Oh…
You want rabbit?
Yes, yes!
When will you come? Madam asked.
Wednesday, I'll come Wednesday.

Over the next few days I ate *croissants, soupe de poisson,*
drank *vin rouge, vin blanc, vin rosé, espresso* and
Evian – lots of Evian.

Wednesday morning, first thing out I bought *l'Express*
et petit dejeuner on *Rue Sévign*é
then wandered past Madam's petit bistro
Would she remember?
And, there she was sweeping the sidewalk
chairs still atop tables.

Will you still make the rabbit? I asked.
I was by the market already and bought one.
How do you want it?
After several choices we agreed, *not with cream*
or *moutard* but simply in its own juices.
We'll see you at eight.

All day looking at paintings in *le Louvre*
window-shopping around *Le Marais*
jogging through *Jardin des Luxembourg*
chatting with a waiter at a café near Bastille

I thought, *Lapin!*
Where would I find a fresh rabbit in Manhattan?
And I'd never be capable of cooking the creature
in its own blood for sauce –
one must have wild, healthy, natural blood
and Madam had promised just that.

The bistro was packed for dinner
customers speaking French, Spanish, English,
Italian, all languages Madam spoke.
I was greeted, seated in a banquette   given
a bottle of wine   no label, no cork
a clear jelly jar glass, basket of bread – no butter:
napkin, knife, fork, spoon for the sauce.
You want a first course? Madam asked
and answered, *No.*
Rabbit is enough, and vanished.

I listened to Madam's friends, watched
them eat, a chunk of bread a piece of sausage
several *cornichons*; watched the women
sitting near Madam, eat ladle-full upon ladle-full
of hearty winter *cassoulet*; watched
the cat roam from one end of the tiny dining room
to the other end, roam with great liberty
a wild beast   searching, on the hunt.

When my pot and dish arrived – Madam lifted the lid
clouds of steam escaped, perfuming my every pore.
She spooned out enough to fill the shallow bowl, and
slowly, I cleaned the bones dry of every tender morsel
sucked the marrow from each vertebra, knowing
bliss, knowing I'd never see Madam again.

She would probably move south with Gertrude
and Artaud (their cat), open a bistro or *auberge*
grow still older…but for now   she was my Paris
just beyond my window, past the waddling ducks
stitched on the hem of the white lace curtains
past the balcony, down my street, around the corner
from Place St. Catherine, Le Marais
where blood soaked the cobblestones
through the centuries   but for now
this dinner, this rabbit was making history
and remembered – breathes life into memory.

This Too Is Avignon

A young man with espresso-stained lips
blows smoke rings under the café awning
where I take cover from hailstones
watch the sway of hips in leather and jeans
watch all the stranded, thrown together
without introduction   holding flashlights
matches, candles, *Bic* lighters
brightening this ancient town gone black.

Beneath my slicker I scurry   search
for a room, *Please just one night...*
The proprietress shows me the smallest room
I've ever seen. A bed and sink.
I throw open the shutters   let in August's humidity
pull the bed sheets to my neck, wait
for the dampness to depart. It doesn't.
Morning breaks through   fills the little cell;
my body is a sea of welts.
At a café table, the streets now dry
I read *le Journal's* headline:
6 American Tourists Murdered in Their Beds.
I eat my croissant, drink my espresso, breathe
the perfume of cypress trees   try to forgive.

Foxtails, et cetera

She vowed to learn the names of all the grasses
where she walked and slept
the yellows, greens, the purple reed, blue grama
and the rest   like mistresses revealing
undergarments when the moment's right.

Yes, she'd study the trees, or at least the ones
giving shade to her days and nights
those under which she'd sit and wander
in her mind, drift into infinity, down aisles
of tall, stately pines, poplars, aspen, a universe
into which she'd disappear   as they bowed
in the wind
or fold like palms in prayer above her head.

But what of the clouds, birds, and insects beyond
Magpies and Dragonflies (those
even she might know) unlike
the Wild Carrot Wasp or Willow Sphinx
unlike the minerals deep in marshland soil
rich with mushrooms, scary in their hues, like
the skins of snakes: rust, lime, oxblood red
pigments like those searched for by painters
to fill their frames with Saskatoons and Fairy bells
with Prairie buttercups and Pussytoes, berries,
blossoms, vibrant as life: delicious and deadly?

She needed to begin, find charts, books on species
phylums, but wait, what was that aria she just heard?
She needed to know, learn composers' names
beyond Mozart, Strauss, Stravinsky.
She didn't want to overlook all the schools of architecture
the forms of verse she loved but did not know by heart.
Ashamed, she needed to confess (if only to herself)
she didn't know her favorite tea – was it Ceylon? Or
the wine she liked to drink – Syrah?

And what of her beloved kitchen tools
used regularly but without a proper name, not
just thingy or whatchamacallit
or the dozens of elaborate fonts designed through the ages
methods of printing: lithograph, serigraph – et cetera
et cetera would no longer do.

Camden, Maine

We stood in the kitchen, back from the beach
thighs gritty with sand

swim suits drying on nails, milk simmering
on the wood stove

hair falling   wet, tangling down our backs
your cat nuzzling our legs.

We spun each other around, like children
dizzying ourselves for fun

supporting each other against tumbling
tumbling against one another.

We were young then, very young
(though we didn't know it) & sunny as the day.

Flying Home

I.

The flight was late, but the tour leader promised
he'd get the fish to the church on time.
They'd been fishing, the church group, and now
were packed in (like fish) on a plane back to Minnesota.
And, though everything had been militarily arranged
the timing timed, the Northern pike, walleye,
Artic grayling, and rainbow trout needed to get in the fridge.
They should still be froze by the time we get 'um to the church.

Proclaim the pain of God! a woman exclaimed
to anyone who'd listen, as she sat down next to me
on American 908 between Saskatoon and Minneapolis.
Silver earrings, miniature Jesuses
nailed to intricately carved crosses pivoted
this way and that as the proselytizer swung her head.
Her handbag bore a plastic bumper sticker
more often seen on Winnebagos and 18-wheelers:
Abortion Is Not Healthcare!
I ordered vodka, no ice, slice of lemon or lime.
Sorry, love, no lemon or lime, informed the airline attendant.

II.

You'll find everything at the mall
the taxi driver from the airport
to the Saskatoon bus terminal, assured me.
He'd recently won a contest:
*Just pulled the lid off a Coca-Cola bottle, mailed it in
and lo and behold, me and my parents we won a trip
to Disney World!   Didn't like it much, but
the parents they liked it swell   never been
out of Saskatchewan so it was good for them.
Me, I know the States – Ohio, Denver. Denver's cool.*

III.
Reductions! Reductions! Reductions!
Bras, sneakers, lawn chairs, pearl pendants
carbines. Three floors. Blinding lights.
Loud "easy listening" music, and a food court
the size of Provincetown.
Vacuum-packed sushi, deep-fried tacos, pizza
permeated every pore. I browsed "Thread Bare"
everything for the embroiderer, crewler, needle-pointer
every color thread, every weight.   I roamed
the Arctic air-conditioned atrium until my bus departure
for Muenster and the monastery.

IV.
That first day, I studied the Benedictine monks
their glide-like stride. In and out of rooms and corridors
around orchards and gravel parking lots. Silently
these men in full-length robes the color of rich dark soil
tended cauliflower, potatoes, corn, tomatoes, pears
apples, herbs lovingly turned into sumptuous meals
by women cutting, stirring, scrambling, baking, broiling.

I strolled up and down between the flowerbeds
like evenly dissected parts on a child's head of hair;
the perennial garden was Brother Michael's creation
his domain; the root cellar, wine making and
computer labs his fellow brothers nurtured.

V.
On a midday walk I met a stranger
walking her blue-eyed sled dog along the road
simply called the "black top," meaning,
it wasn't dirt or gravel.
You've come to God's country, she assured me
You're lucky to be in Muenster, God's country!

Here, men, women and children flock
for the annual pilgrimage and to touch God;
they travel miles and miles in SUVs, vans
and big purple tour buses; believers
reserving rooms a year in advance
to be near the holy "Mount" where "she" resides
she the child saint. *If you are one of the lucky,*
the stranger had informed, *God touches you*
leaves some mark.

VI.
Now, I was heading home
on a flight with the promise of a bag of chips
and not a lemon or lime slice in sight.
Everything dimmed inside the plane, but I knew
"The Mount" was rockin' with music. I'd seen posters
on the walls outside the cafeteria
on the post office bulletin board
on the front door of the supermarket
next to a sign: CANDLE MAKING WORKSHOP.

I was missing the concert
and I'd miss the Polka Fest too
the summer's second biggest attraction
the first being a guided tour
of the province's largest   fertilizer manufacturer.

VII.
Through time zones, the woman slept
silver Jesus earrings quivering; in her lap
lay an open magazine – the cover advertising:
Holy Action Heroes: Kids Love 'Em.

I read my book, a love story about WWI
unwed mothers and their soldiers
long gone to mulch for the French countryside.
Beneath my thin polyester Delta blanket
my fingers mingled, secretly praying
for a safe landing on familiar turf.

Paradise Island

In a ravenous half-clothed state
I jumped my Caribbean patio gate
pursuing a coconut down the road
squishing lizards dodging toads;
apologizing to the plant
I scaled its shingled trunk –
it was me against the fruit.

Tearing and pulling in the night
it finally shook loose   and
with reptilian speed I scurried
to my chamber's outdoor court
one leg then the next I landed
right foot in the butter, left one in the cup
(damn that luncheon tray).

Now to crack the furry nut.
So, at 3 a.m. I sent that fruit flying
against the Turkish tiled porch, but
as I watched my meal
bouncing back and forth
it'd only lost a hair or two, otherwise
completely there intact.
Once more I waged war
throwing full force against the floor
and just like Humpty-Dumpty
it cracked in several pieces.

About to feast on juice and meat
no knife or fork could be found
so from the closet I retrieved a hanger
and freeing it of its twisted shape
cross-legged upon my bed – I ate.

Bear Harbor, CA

Had I known the danger – would I have gone?
Never! Sometimes it's best   to not know
but to follow like a hound on a scent
despite harrowing twists and hairpin turns
the ominous thoughts of catastrophe
knowing
it's usually better to keep going
for the promise
          to ourselves.

IV.

War

They do it for themselves
these women wearing sheer stockings
shoes dusted of rubble that had been
their stoves, bookshelves, booties
crocheted for the first, second
now dead
in rubble they walk through
these women in shoes dusted off
and stockings, carrying their lives
in sheets they once pressed crisp
flung across a wedding bed
memories of their first night still bright
in their minds
they cling to like scalloped sheets
in their hands
cling to a community of souls
reaching deep   down
in a way they never knew
was in them, could never know
was possible, like
their universe gone in a gulp, but
not the bed's memories or
laughter over tables set with "good china"
filled with hot bread, lentil soup, garlic
like a sweet drug, strong   but
not strong enough.

These women walk, have been walking
through centuries through streets
over mountains across deserts, hiding, while
feeding infants from breasts
in name only;
these women remember giddy gossip, remember
where they hid birthday cakes to surprise the innocent.

They are walking still
caring for their last pair of stockings
as one covets a scrap of love letter, the rest
lost in a fire or flood or who knows where.
They covet this luxury not out of vanity, but
for love
of the lost, for sanity, for hope
no matter how sheer, sheerer even
than the air they now breathe.

These stockings, not good for anything, really
not good to hold water or bolster a sinking roof
or heart.
Still, these women   with
faces no longer pink, but gray with shadow
dust off their shoes   slip on their stockings.

Locked-down Zone

After the buildings crumbled
decimating the soul of the streets
the sanity of humanity   shredded
that blue September day   turned night;
after the contents cascaded   from the heavens
over and over   through smoke
dark as night
the images repeating and repeating
incessant torture for the living;
after the survivors folded up like origami
never to feel protected again
never to erase the charred odor of flesh
ever to be claimed –
we resumed in the *locked-down zone*
raw   determined   unstoppable.

Stench

Every day   *yes*, every day
it's painful   because forgetting
is not an option   simply not an option
to forget that day   forget those buildings
that once towered   right *here*   said
This is your home.
Now, when strolling   south on my tree-lined street
every step is a slow rip   painful
a Band-Aid tearing open   again and again   *that* wound

Nurse Practitioner

She is 15 minutes late
says she emailed to let me know
but apologizes profusely anyway.
It is nothing I tell her.

I had to stitch up this guy's butt.
I pour her a glass of ice water.
He had too much crystal and sex.

She is shaken, this woman who treats eunuchs
trans-gender prostitutes, every permutation of those
who do not fit the Male, Female, "Check the box" model.
She does her nursing in Delhi, Cairo, New York City.

I never saw a tear that large, she says.
He was so embarrassed.

She takes out her yellow and orange folders
finds the story – the one about the people of South India
who escape to live in underwater bubbles.
She pays me cash   from money she earns freelance
separate from clinic work –
she inseminates lesbians who recruit male friends.
I'm good with a turkey baster, she says, smiling.

When T returns from Cairo after the revolution
she brings me delicate hand-blown tea glasses
sparkling, full of glitter
as some children believe life will be.

We swim for an hour in the warm current
of her imagination, infinite worlds.
Leaving, she breaks a drinking glass
apologizes profusely, is mortified.
It is nothing, I say. And really,
it is so *nothing*.

Knee Brace

I walk into the waiting room, sit
watch the clock   knowing I'll be late
will need to run, *fast*   despite arthritic knees
and shoes that shred flesh into thin filets
throughout the day.

Two young men enter the waiting room
bring with them August's heat and humidity.
One holds something obscured
wrapped in a floral sheet;
his buff friend wears Adidas
on one foot.
I turn my gaze   but not quick enough
catch a glimpse of a matching Adidas
on his prosthetic leg draped in daisy print.

The attendant brings out my brace,
I thank her.
Mr. Buff looks at me, smiles   says
Great beach day!
And I say *yes*   to *everything*.

Pain Q

She's one of those perfect beauties
skin like porcelain   a luster of dreams
slender and wearing sweat pants, running shoes
a Peruvian knit hat.
She's sitting at a communal table
sipping coffee, eating a croissant
her child on her lap   two small hands
flailing and thrilled with holding his bottle.
Mom removes her hat, colorful earflaps
no longer framing her scull
            chemo-screaming-bald.

No Excuses

I want to paint everything
white   to the bone:
walls floors woodwork

want to move
through the house
my senses   wide open

want to strip the walls
layer from layer
even the ghosts cower

want to rip down ceilings
to the beams   plaster
insulation   nails

want to discard
whatever remains
beyond remains

want to change
the words – *That's the way it is*
can't do anything about it.

Little Town

Here in Reserve, New Mexico   canyons
and wilderness   elk, coyote, wolves
once ran free   reminds me
how bleak *bleak* can be.

Not long ago, wolves was the big issue.
They followed the spotted owl, before the trees got axed
disorienting the birds – turned them homeless:
no food source, no breeding ground.

All our livestock's dying, Lance the rancher tells me.
The law's against us, against us making a living
to feed our kids; that's politics for you.

Yet, hope prevails
through god, liquor and the coming rain.
There's never a line at Reserve's ATM or gas station
and you'll get all the beer a body could want at Willard's.
Willard's got a rockin' bar and pool table
and the best jukebox playing the best Country
Country's got. Willard tells jokes, bad, foul
anti-woman jokes. Cracks himself up.

Curtis the young, *Could be a star*   wrangler
tells Willard   *Buddy, you gotta smile*
at the weight of your body movin' you
through your day, listen to Country
the good Country   and have faith
in that promising sky   ain't nothing else
then shoots three billiard balls into the pocket –
It's good man, all good.

Petit Paradis

Trained as a seamstress, Mom couldn't embroider her dreams.
    for Ora L.

You appear in the oddest places:
outside *Whole Foods* (no longer there)
running along the Hudson River
(that run, so different now
since our city collapsed
into something you'd never recognize).
Stepping down from the bus –
I'm sure I see you, but of course
I don't.

When life swirls around
in chaos, my work remains
a steadying place, you said
about your painting and anchoring.

Here, resting in your corner
at what had been your *petit paradis*
cobbled together year by year
bush by tree by rock
your ashes breathe in every petal
every blade of grass every bit of basil;
your thoughts heard in postcards tumbling
from between pages of poetry and
art books
your touch in hand-stitched rugs
your image everlasting in photos:
on the lawn with new kittens
surrounded by Monet's Oriental poppies
and clematis in Giverny
colorful as your floral blue Chinese coat
(you wore to my wedding)
embroidered as your mother never could
you remain, as ever   *defiant*.

Bryant Park

One day I just let go.
Don't know how it happened, but
seeing a broken park chair   a leg undone
from a missing screw   realized
I too was no longer tightly fastened.
Parts had not fallen off into a heap
something gel-like, cohesive
like the netting covering the brain
filmy and delicate yet tight and strong
held things together
in place, *sort of.*

Still, I was disassembling:
structure existed, but I wondered:
What if I *really* came apart
pieces klunking on the ground
an arm here, a foot there
teeth out of nowhere?

So I said, *why not*   let go
gave in   sat on a bench, watched
scrubby vines curl up the trees
in winter   pushing forward
without hesitation.

Szymborska Says...

Don't feel guilty says Szymborska
snakes and alligators and condors
don't feel guilty for attacking
for severing the vocal cords or
removing the hearts from their prey
it's part of their nature, part of the game plan
created long before they hatched from their shells.
Go, says Szymborska, go and become
whom you were meant to become; *go*
persevere – follow your pulse, and
the reason you're on this earth.

Girl

No clothes is how we like each other best
slight of hip, swish of curve.

Hey girl, bring your body over here
sit on my lap the way you never did
way back when. Sit here, right *here*
& ride me   *ride me wild*, through cotton
lace & flesh   through creaking & shifting
through noises filling the air shaft, sweet
as your fingertips to my mouth.
     Gallop girl
under full moon rising   *rising*
in a country of our creation, our mountains
our rivers.

Sit high, ride me low   ride me *deep*
through fears & years   through, *Hey*
no way!
through love & anger & the subtle task
of learning how to take our separate journeys
do the things we need to do, because
we believe in transformation, believe
that maybe, we'll get it going, get it together
get it.

And still, we know there's no settling
we're nomads following our senses
and a chorus   only the angels can hear.

Caught on Video

Toes curled over the edge of the high dive
Trish balanced
        testing   with short   quick   jumps
the spring.

Her red nylon racer's suit glistened
drenched in sunlight
        as she calculated her   arc.

T didn't look her age
but vacillated between twelve and   twenty.
A student
    triathlon champion   volunteer worker.

Flawlessly   with graceful bounce
she leapt   airborne   smiling
and jackknifed

        into the empty pool.

Café de l'Opéra

The two had become one
even their silver hair curled identically
around their faces   just covering their earlobes
that seemed perked towards each other
ready to listen   to respond.

Her blue-grey eyes sparkled kaleidoscopically
so when looking closely one could see
her travels, children, lost joys, accumulated sorrows
of living so long, watching the years depart.

He sat quietly, reserved behind thick black frames
wearing charcoal grey from neck to foot;
his face resembled a weathered landscape
still changing.   He was monumentally
in love with her   mesmerized
by this lovely lady, wearing a silk scarf
creatively tied around her visibly aging neck.

The two spoke rapidly accentuating with their hands;
her slender fingers, ringed with silver and amethyst
danced through the air; his fingers, stout, knobby and
without adornment   moved powerfully
in precise expressive gestures   touching hers
        in mid-air.

Like two jungle birds, companions for life
dignified, courageous   paired
they push through the unknown
move into the future.

Unbuttoned

The nape of your neck lures me
fine blonde down, soft wisps   barely visible
along the narrow curve of vertebrae   *rising*
from India-ink-blue shirt   buttons up the back
soft flesh emerging above scoop of collar.

Have you forgotten to fasten the top and middle buttons?
Or maybe they've come undone from too much tugging
on a blouse no longer the proper fit.
Your flesh and random freckles keep me transfixed
on the white marble color and lotion-smooth texture
of skin where the strand of sea pearls sits.

Further down, bra strap appears where silk shirt   open
like a garden gate into some other world yet to be seen
invites whomever happens to notice   *in*.
That horizontal stretch of strap, keeping young breasts up
in place   playing hide and seek   depending
on your stance   arm over the chair's back
arms crossed or straightening your pose
permitting shirt to fall falsely   closed.

Your feather haircut, clear nail polish, pumps
businesswoman's *Timex*   speak one language
but   when wrist appears   flesh the hue of neck
and back   I revisit sea pearls and freckles
know I'm captured   provoked.

Has it been your intention, this invitation?
What pulls me to you?
Not your choice of silk blouse or navy jacket
arranged in repose   now being lifted
placed over shoulders (did you feel my penetrating gaze?)
but your unflinching attention to tonight's invited readers
and ability to sit   so unaware of yourself
becoming undressed in public.

Amtrak Home

From the window of the Amtrak train
a young girl sits looking out on the landscape
impoverished and exhilarating.

She sits inside a middle-aged woman's body
but *trust me* – she is no more than 13
and loves the speed, the blur, the mystery
of possibilities that are still out there
still unfolding   as the journey to Philadelphia
unfolds on this New Year's day   like that afternoon
she wore a borrowed dress   black & white
Mod print   so short and flowy
feminine for Jonathan's indie film
chosen to go to New York
as she would do years later
after the director cut his long hair
gave up his Communist affiliation, turned Social Worker,
after the world turned upside down and inside out
as the world does   over and over
like people
    if we're resilient.

Sheepskin Memories

We took Amtrak   from Penn Station, Philly
to Penn Station, Manhattan   walked

on a sunny Fall day   to the Village
where my sister lived and attended art school.

We meandered along St. Mark's Place
the thumping, incessant 24/7 rhythm and green haze

enveloping my mother and me   as it did
and does today   as I sit on a bench with cup of coffee

across from the sheepskin shop
where she and I laughed, ridiculed those huge coats

on my small frame   lost beneath sheep curls
that would keep me warm, cozy through college

New Hampshire, New York, Minnesota, Montreal, Maine.
She was practical, living in the moment – and *always* fashionable.

Looking in a mirror was not vanity   it was an *imperative*
penetrating beyond fabric, pleats, accessories;

if you didn't look, scrutinize – you were flawed;
you didn't want to be flawed   and yet – you were.

Applesauce Jars
for Peaches

When we buried our time capsules
beneath your cabin
we buried some of ourselves.
We both included poems.
Yours was about infants
flying, flying, flying
out of cribs
into the arms of nothing.
Mine was about finally being released
from between my thighs.
You inserted a joint of homegrown Colombian
plus a Polaroid of your snake
and hummingbird tattoos.
I chose an ounce of dried statice
and a photo of myself
dressed in Victorian camisole and skirt.
We each stuffed one brassiere cup;
I folded in a pink dancing shoe
you squeezed in a rock group's tape.
On the top, you placed a black silk scarf;
I dropped in a strand of pearls.
Girls you know, will be girls.

Beyond Bodies
for Sue

Our reflections in Wanamaker's mirror
on Saturday afternoons in Philly
is how I remember us: your chest
squished in, overflowing bikini cups
way too tiny for all your wealth;
my slim curve of waist, naked,
an hour glass of flesh
invited hands   and dancing to bongos
on the Jersey shore.
My rhythm and moves attracted boys
to cut in on you and dance with me;
but your confidence and breasts got them
to ask for a date.

Years out of high school, after college
after we moved from Philly to New York City
we found ourselves
at a 40% off lingerie sale
on Thompson Street   where we *both* live
far from Susquehanna Avenue
and the shopping center where we hung out
spent too much money on uncomfortable shoes
and cheap eye make-up.
My waist is thicker, your breasts well…
still, the decades haven't changed us
not *really*.

Why I Read You

Your poems   dark   as coconut shell
sweet   as a baby's belly
able to kiss   ready to quench
a long thirst   quell   the heart
like Billie and Bessie
deep, hard and   *speakin'*
the truth.

Dr. Ken

I am wracked with guilt.
I know I should floss, but
I'm not compliant.

My dentist reminds me,
You need to floss, that's why
you're getting blood.
I mention Susan, a friend
and also Kenny's patient
though she's long overdue.

She has great gums, he says.
I think, but don't say, No wonder,
her days are free to *floss floss floss.*

No denying, Sue's got *great* gums,
spectacular even, while mine, well
are turning mushy as we speak.

As my dentist scrapes, upping the nitrous oxide
decay grows more interesting.
My *Leica*, with a different lens, would capture
the organisms proliferating in my mouth
monsters amongst eroding monoliths;
it's *all* in the lens.
I leave numb and giddy with my goody-bag:
toothbrush, toothpaste, floss.

Once home, I arrange the spools of white floss
around the apartment: on the bookshelf, near the couch
on the bedroom bureau, in the kitchen
near the chopping board - reminders:
my gums are me
     it's good to have teeth.

Hyacinths

something dramatic   was on the horizon
keeping her on edge   pushing
to a decision   absolute resolute
persistent   through paralysis
beyond   the wreckage.

Madeleine Beckman is a poet, fiction, and nonfiction writer. She has received awards from among other institutions, the Poetry Society of America, the New York Foundation for the Arts, and the Irish Arts Council of Ireland. Her fellowships include Fundación Valparaíso (ES), Ragdale, Virginia Center for the Creative Arts, and the Tyrone Guthrie Center (IE).

Her poetry collection, *Dead Boyfriends,* was first published by Linear Arts Press in 1998, and was reissued by Limoges Press in 2012. Her second collection, *No Roadmap, No Brakes,* was published in 2015 by Red Bird Chapbooks.

She has organized readings and appearances with among others, Paul Muldoon, Tom Lux, James Lasdun, and Colm Toibin. Her published interviews with poets include Stanley Kunitz, Seamus Heaney, Galway Kinnell, Audre Lorde, and Jean Valentine.

She is a Contributing Reviewer for the *Bellevue Literary Review,* and Contributing Editor for *Agora,* the arts journal of New York University School of Medicine. Madeleine received her B.A. and M.A. from New York University, and her M.F.A. from Fairleigh Dickinson University. She teaches at New York University School of Medicine, Division of Medical Humanities, and privately.
http://www.writedown.com

www.ingramcontent.com/pod-product-compliance
Lightning Source LLC
LaVergne TN
LVHW011211080426
835508LV00007B/733